Plug Fishing

For Steelhead

By Mike Laverty

"I have fished with Mike on several occasions with success! He is an accomplished plug fisherman. His book is a must for all steelheaders who wish to learn or sharpen their angling skills."

—Buzz Ramsey
Professional Fisherman

A Frank Amato

PORTLAND

Acknowledgments

I would like to thank all the fishermen who have fished with me over the years. Those who took me when I was a young boy and those who joked with me about my seriousness and organization. All of you have contributed to this book in some way.

The efforts of Dave Schamp, Troy Gusick, Dan Kern and many others in editing my manuscript cannot be matched. Thank you all for your time, honesty and encouragement to complete this process. Your fishing friendships and netting proficiency can never be replaced or forgotten.

A special thanks to my beautiful wife, Heidi, the "Czar" of the personal computer, for spending many evenings in solitude as I worked at the kitchen table. Last, but not least, thank you Dad for going fishing.

Published in 1994 by Frank Amato Publications, Inc.
P.O. Box 82112, Portland, Oregon 97282
ISBN: 1-878175-92-0
UPC: 0-66066-00173-3
Front and Back Cover Photos: Jim Schollmeyer
Book Design: Charlie Clifford
Drawings by: Jonah Edera
Printed in Hong Kong
1 3 5 7 9 10 8 6 4 2

Contents

Acknowledgments   **2**
Introduction   **4**

Chapter 1
Why Plug?   **6**

Chapter 2
Boat Set Up   **8**

Chapter 3
Rod & Reel Selection   **11**

Chapter 4
Types of Plugs   **15**

Chapter 5
Proper Tuning of Plugs   **18**

Chapter 6
Hook Set Ups   **25**

Chapter 7
Designing Your Own Colors and Patterns   **32**

Chapter 8
Choosing the Right Plug   **35**

Chapter 9
Proper Rigging   **43**

Chapter 10
Fishing Your Plugs   **46**

Chapter 11
Curtain of Death   **53**

Chapter 12
Fish the Flats   **55**

Chapter 13
Plugging Hazards   **58**

Chapter 14
Maneuvering with Ease   **60**

Chapter 15
Fish Others!   **62**

Introduction

This book is intended for the novice fisherman as well as those with experience with the art of fishing plugs. It provides insight and tips for all who want to improve their steelheading technique. For purposes of this book I define plugging as, fishing by method of back trolling with a drift boat using Hot Shots, Wiggle Warts, Flatfish, Kwikfish and other plugs.

Through numerous years of fishing for steelhead, I have learned many things about fishing with plugs. The knowledge shared in *Plug Fishing for Steelhead* is derived from my experience in fishing diving lures and fishing with other plug fishermen, whom I consider to be some of the best around. Of course my opinion is subjective and I realize there are others out there who are also good plug fishermen that could have put this book together. I don't know it all, nor do I consider myself the best at this fishing technique but simply the deliverer of valuable information to help others catch more fish using this method.

My experience with plug fishing comes from the need to incorporate a technique that allows a novice steelheader a better chance to catch fish. I enjoy taking my father fishing and despite good intentions he is not quite the athlete he once was, nor are his skills and coordination the same. In other words, my dad is a terrible drift fisherman. (Sorry Dad). He can bird nest a spinning reel! Because I enjoyed the companionship of my father, I needed to find an effective method to catch fish and keep him from becoming frustrated. Plugging was the obvious choice. I saw other fishermen fish this way and used to swear at them because they were always fishing my boondoggling water. Another reason for developing the plugging technique began after I moved to the Portland area from the central coast and started to fish Tillamook area rivers. I was introduced to a different world of steelhead fishing, the world of crowds. This meant I had to plug many seldom fished areas of rivers, as bank fishermen were everywhere else. Plugging allowed me to thoroughly fish areas and produce fish in sections of rivers that would not be classified as classic steelhead water and for that reason left void of bank fishermen.

A note to the skeptic: There are many reasons to fish plugs. Along with providing an effective technique for those who are not skilled in drift fishing, plugging is also a great way to get people into their first steelhead. It provides experience in fighting a fish correctly, including use of the current and learning how to properly net a fish. Yes, people can learn this catching their first steelhead by drift fishing too but it has been my experience that beginning steelhead fishermen have a better chance of catching fish while in a drift boat pulling plugs.

Drift fishing while standing on the bank, or even in a boat, the techniques take considerable time to master. There are a couple of reasons why I feel fishing plugs provides a fish catching advantage to the beginner; one is that while fishing with a beginner in a boat pulling plugs, the opportunity is doubled or tripled if you allow the rookie to take whichever rod the fish strikes. The time spent actually fishing with hooks in the water is greatest when fishing plugs.

As I began to put more time and effort into the technique of plugging, I found there is a lot more to it if you want to consistently take fish by this method. It is true there are suicide fish who hit any plug regardless of its presentation, color and size but to consistently take fish with plugs there are many items that need attention. Many say that pulling plugs is an uncomplicated way of fishing, I disagree. The remainder of this book is devoted to addressing the needs of fishing plugs and providing valuable information to improve your chances of consistent success.

Plug Fishing for Steelhead addresses fishing plugs from a drift boat. The contents are also applicable to fishing plugs from jet sleds as the back trolling technique is the same regardless of the method of power, human or other.

5

1
Why Plug?

All smiles, Dave Schamp with a beautiful chrome 17 pound Wilson River steelhead. Dave enticed the big, spring native hen to take a size 30 Hot Shot that was white with a red head.

There are five popular ways to fish for steelhead; 1.) drift fishing with drift bobbers and bait; 2.) fishing with spinners; 3.) jig fishing; 4.) fly fishing; and 5.) fishing with plugs. I know that there are others but these are surely the most popular. All five methods have their advantages and disadvantages which others in the fishing world have thoroughly discussed. As a means of catching steelhead, plug fishing rates near the top. In my opinion the advantages of plugs outweigh the other methods. When back trolled by drift boat, sled or side planer, a correctly chosen, tuned and presented plug worked carefully through a piece of steelhead holding water will give you quality fishing time. How long the plug hangs over a piece of water is at the oarsman's control. Unlike any other technique, when you fish plugs you can have a hook in the water from daylight to dark.

Why steelhead strike plugs is somewhat debatable. Many believe in the theory (myself included) that steelhead, once they have entered freshwater on their spawning migration, become territorial in nature. Thus, as the plug, or plugs in most cases, are being back trolled down to holding steelhead they interpret the plug as an intruder into their territory. It is common for steelhead to strike plugs at the top of riffles. This happens because back trolled plugs have pushed the fish downriver to a point where the fish does not want to descend down the riffle any further only to forge and expend valuable energy to ascend the riffle again. Many fishermen believe that the steelhead's curiosity leads it to strike. I do not discount any theory, but I do know the technique of plugging does cause fish to strike.

Unlike other methods when fished downriver the hooks on plugs are facing upriver away from snags and reducing the chance for a hang up. This reason alone greatly improves your fishing time because there is no need to constantly retie rigs that have broken off. All steelhead fishermen know the misery of tying up a rig with frozen fingers.

2
Boat Set Up

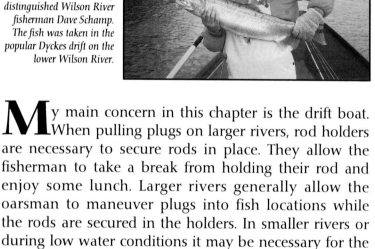

Another notch for the size 35 blue pirate Hot Shot of distinguished Wilson River fisherman Dave Schamp. The fish was taken in the popular Dyckes drift on the lower Wilson River.

My main concern in this chapter is the drift boat. When pulling plugs on larger rivers, rod holders are necessary to secure rods in place. They allow the fisherman to take a break from holding their rod and enjoy some lunch. Larger rivers generally allow the oarsman to maneuver plugs into fish locations while the rods are secured in the holders. In smaller rivers or during low water conditions it may be necessary for the front seat fisherman to hold the rod. This will allow for easy repositioning of the rod to maneuver the plug through small tough–to–hit pockets or slots which hold fish.

Keeping rods under your feet or secured by other precarious methods inhibits your ability to read the rod tip and may restrict the performance of the rod. I have seen rods that were not secured properly or were held inattentively pulled out of the boat. Rod holders like those made by Tempress are excellent and can be mounted most any place on the boat. I recommend removing the white plastic rod lock as it is not needed.

Its removal will prevent attempted use by the novice.

Considerations should be made to placement of rod holders. When mounting rod holders make sure the support mount will allow for placement and easy turning of the holders for adjustment and removal. Keep location of heaters in mind, those under the fly deck especially. I have seen many rod holders that cannot be used once mounted because the heater melts the bottom of the holder or burns the cork rod handle. Make functional and observational checks before drilling any holes.

Common places to secure rod holders are on the left and right gunnels, left and right of knee braces on the fly deck and on side trays behind the front seat, in front of the oarsman. The number of rod holders should equal the maximum number of fishermen that fish in your boat. Placement of rod holders is important because the oarsman needs to view the rod tips of all rods at any time. A view of the rod tips allows the oarsman to determine if plugs are working properly. Sit on the oarsman's seat during the mounting process to get an idea of the best rod holder placement. Your perspective changes when viewing things from the oarsman seat.

Propane heaters also need planning before placement. If you are purchasing a new boat and plan to have the heater system plumbed in before floor boards are installed, research placement areas. The standard area for attachment of the heater head is the foot rest below the boat's fly deck. I have found that placing the heater head further back, underneath the fly deck, will produce heat like an oven to the fly deck above and sustains the heat as the surrounding metal is heated. This causes no problems for the boat's construction. Willie Boats manufactures a forced air system below the fly that is operated by electric fan. Make sure all heater mount locations allow for seat adjustments and removal. Heater system plumbing is often overlooked in designing and choosing options for your drift boat purchase. When purchasing a new drift boat keep in mind most drift boat manufacturers can build to suit your needs, it just costs you money!

3
Rod & Reel Selection

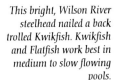

This bright, Wilson River steelhead nailed a back trolled Kwikfish. Kwikfish and Flatfish work best in medium to slow flowing pools.

Fishing is done with many different types of rods and reels. To maximize your efforts, different fishing techniques require carefully selected, specialized rods and reels. The drift fisherman has many choices in rods, for example length, stiffness and construction material all vary with each rod. The same holds true for the plug fisherman. My recommendation is a one piece rod in the seven to eight foot range with a light tip and heavy butt. A one piece, shorter rod is sensitive, strong and has plenty of back bone to fight a fish. A finger trigger is also a nice feature to have. The one piece rod is great in the boat and truck because it does not have to be broken down every trip. A light tip on a plug rod is necessary to read the action of the plug being fished and a rod with too heavy a tip will not allow the plug to perform at its optimum. The plug's ability to dive and wiggle freely is key to enticing a strike from steelhead. Reading the plug for proper action and the ability to determine if the plug is weeded up is less obvious with a heavier tipped rod. In theory the larger the fish

John Turley poses with a Wilson River hatchery fish. The fish was taken from a flat passed over by previous fishermen.

the larger the plug you should choose to fish. Many who run plugs during Chinook season choose a larger plug, for the larger fish, which requires a heavier rod. Major rod building companies have designed and produced rods specifically for plugging. Choose your plug rod (or rods) carefully. Consider the size of the fish you are after, the type and sizes of plugs you are going to run the majority of time and the amount of money you want to spend. My two recommendations for plug rods are the Talon SHS 761 or Fenwick LP76C. These rods are in the working man's price range and meet all the criteria you expect in a rod. For those who have extra money to spend the Loomis HS 9000 is a great choice, I consider it to be the Excaliber of plug rods.

Another alternative is to make your own rod. Although in the last few years the components necessary for a quality rod have become almost as expensive as a prebuilt rod, the joy and satisfaction of creating and building your own rod cannot be matched. I have fishing friends with garages full of expensive, first class store bought graphite rods and on the river the rod that's in their rod holder they made themselves from a fiberglass blank. Many consider the fiberglass plug rod to be the best as it provides great flexibility with the sensitivity needed for good plug action.

I prefer to paint two to four small fluorescent stripes on the tip of my plug rods or include fluorescent wraps on my handmade rods. In the early and late hours of the day when light is low these stripes allow you to read the rod tip without developing eyestrain. It seems most of the new graphite rods are dark in color and against a dark gray sky it is difficult to see the rod tip.

The preferred choice for reels are those in the level wind category. Although spinning reels work they inhibit your ability to measure the amount of line coming off the spool. A good drag and anti-backlash system is a must for a plug reel. These systems come into use not only when fighting fish but also in the adjustment of give when a fish strikes a plug. Drag which is too tight when fishing with light test (six to eight pound) has the potential for breaking with a fish on. The drag should be adjusted to match the line used. The heavier the pound test the tighter the drag adjustment should be. Choose a level wind reel with a line capacity of 150 to 180 yards of eight to twelve pound test monofilament. Depending on the size of spool it may be necessary to use a backing of Dacron. It is important to note the date new line is put on a spool and include the pound test. I have found it wise to also include the brand name of the line. With the amount of new ultra-thin monofilament on the market it is difficult to determine what pound test the line is simply by looking. A great way to keep track of desired line information is to write the information down on a small piece of masking tape and place it under the reel seat.

I have found Fenwick's new Riverline in twelve pound test works very well. The line stays soft over time and continued use and has a diameter that does not inhibit plug action. The larger the diameter, the more the plug will be affected by the line's drag in water. Another line that I recommend is Maxima Ultra green in the same test. An important criteria for choosing line for a plug reel is color. It is imperative that you are able to see where your line enters the water, a difficult task in choppy water from a heavy current or wind and low light conditions. The perfect plug line is one you can see but the fish cannot. I have experimented with a few easy-to-see lines, and yes, you can see them with ease but I have experienced less fish strikes with their use, while opposite rods with darker line produced numerous strikes. Using clear leader will help eliminate this problem, this will be covered later in the book.

Smaller diameter lines allow the plug's action in water to be enhanced due to less resistance. A small diameter line with great strength is what a plug fisherman should look for.

4
Types of Plugs

It pays to experiment with different plug color combinations. Sometimes steelhead love plugs with a clown colored finish.

There are many plugs to choose from in your local sporting goods store or tackle shop that catch steelhead. I have found five brands to be most popular in producing steelhead for the plug fisherman. The Hot Shot and Kwikfish plug lines manufactured by Luhr–Jensen, Wiggle Wart lines manufactured by Storm, the Helin Flat Fish manufactured by Yakima Bait Company and the Tadpolly manufactured by Heddon. Yes, there are other brands that catch steelhead but these are the most popular and are readily available in a variety of sizes and colors.

Luhr–Jensen's Hot Shot line is the most popular and provides a wide variety of sizes and colors for the plug fisherman to choose from. Several of their Hot Shot sizes and colors were developed strictly with steelhead in mind. Size is determined by number, the smaller the plug size the higher the number. The exception is the SE series which is categorized in ounces, 1/4 ounce, 1/2 ounce and 3/4 ounce. The most popular sizes for steelhead are 25, 30, 35 and 40. Size 25 is the largest of the four and comes with two treble hooks. Hot Shots dive a range of 10 to 18 feet in depth, depending on the size of plug. There are many advantages to fishing Hot Shots when compared to other brand plugs. Changing plugs, when a different color or size is called for, is not time consuming nor is it a cumbersome process. I have found most Hot Shots purchased off the shelf swim true and require little or no additional tuning. All Hot Shots come with a clip (round eye snap) that attaches to your main line or leader. The snap can be opened and closed easily to change to a different plug. Sizes 30 and 40 in the Hot Shot series are nonrattle plugs, rattles are standard in sizes 25 and 35.

The Storm Wiggle Wart comes in five sizes, Pee Wee Wart, Wee Steelie Wart, Wee Wart and the Magnum Wiggle Wart. The Wee Wart and the Wiggle Wart are the most popular for steelhead. The Magnum Wiggle Wart seems to be too large in this arena but has been proven to catch Chinook in the larger rivers. The Wiggle Wart line comes in a wide variety of colors and color combinations. Making changes with a Wiggle Wart is a little cumbersome and time consuming if fished like instructed from the package, this requires you to cut and retie for the change. This situation can be corrected, without affecting performance of the plug, using a Hot Shot round eyed snap. The Pee Wee Wart and Wee Steelie Wart are manufactured with the line-tie eyelet recessed into a hole on the bill of the plug. To compensate for this Storm Lures has added a figure eight-shaped pivoting eyelet to the line-tie eyelet. Using a Hot Shot snap on the pivoting eyelet does work but has some affects on the plugs action. I recommend for plugs this size tying your line directly to the pivoting eyelet.

The Helin Flat Fish manufactured by Yakima Bait Company and Kwikfish by Luhr-Jensen are virtually the same to the plug fisherman. The sizes available and the swimming action of the plugs are almost identical. These plugs are gaining popularity and are a common choice for Chinook when wrapped with a sardine fillet. When being back trolled for steelhead from a drift boat I have found the most popular sizes to be in the 2 1/2 to 3 1/4 inch range or from 5.5 to 8.5 grams on the weight scale. Each brand has a different model number for the plug's weight and length. These plugs are the most finicky to run from a drift boat because they do not run well in all types of water. They also tend to require a great deal of tuning to run properly.

The Tadpolly manufactured by Heddon is also a popular steelhead plug. The size for catching steelhead is 2 7/8 inch, 1/2 ounce. Although limited in color and patterns, those available catch fish. The Tadpolly fishes well in slow to medium current conditions.

5
Proper Tuning of Plugs

A true-running, properly tuned plug will dive straight down. It is essential that all plugs are checked regularly.

Keeping the plug you are fishing properly tuned, regardless of the brand, is possibly the single most important factor. For some reason steelhead will not strike a poorly tuned plug. I suspect the action and vibrating song produced by an out–of–tune plug does not represent an intruder to the steelhead as a correctly tuned plug does. To determine if your plug is tuned throw it over the side of the boat with a few feet of slack line. Once the plug has begun to dive, take the slack out of your line and give the plug a test pull. Do this by forcing the rod tip back towards the stern of your drift boat at a nine o'clock position and drag the plug through the water where you can observe its action. This generally takes four or five times to determine which direction or side the plug is running toward. A true-running, properly tuned plug will dive straight down. A plug that is out of tune will not dive straight down but will dive off to one side or the other. This action if not corrected will often cause the plug to flip up onto the water's surface once the plug is out below the boat. This is especially true when fishing Flat Fish or Kwikfish because these plugs have a horizontal action in the water. An out–of–tune plug will also make it difficult to run several plugs abreast as the plugs often tangle into each other. Unnecessary line twist is another concern avoided when the plug is properly tuned.

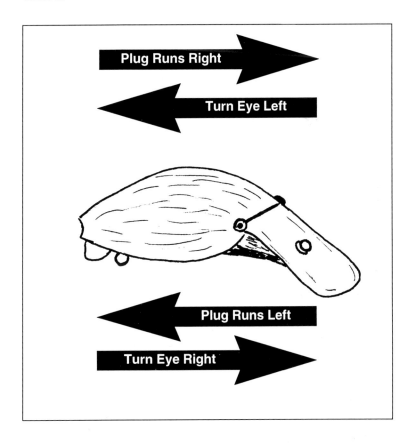

Once the running direction of the plug is determined, hand tuning is ready to begin. The tuning process is a little different with each brand of plug. With Hot Shots, Flat Fish and Kwikfish the problem solving process is similar.

The first item to check is the screw eye on the bill of these plugs. With the plug bill facing you check to make sure the screw eye is in line with the middle of the plug (where a nose would appear between the plugs eyes), if the screw eye is turned off to one side or the other you may have found the problem. Keep in mind this does not work for every plug, some will be out-of-tune even when the screw eye is straight with the middle of the plug. A plug with an off centered screw eye requires you to turn the screw eye in the opposite direction the plug is running towards. Do this in small increments with a pair of needle nose pliers, then test pull the plug and adjust until the plug dives straight down giving you the necessary fish catching action and vibrating song you want. Other items to check are the screw eyes where the hooks are attached, care should be taken to make sure these are in a straight line from front to back. A hook screw eye turned perpendicular to the plug's center line will create enough resistance in the water to cause a problem with the plug's action. This effect can be doubled if the plug has two hooks like the Flat Fish, Kwikfish and Tadpolly.

Remember with Flat Fish and Kwikfish to remove the pivoting eyelet from the screw eye and replace it with a Hot Shot clip. In tuning Kwikfish and Flat Fish additional weight is often needed in front of the plug to keep it from rolling back up on top of the water. The method and distance above the plug varies. I have found two methods to work successfully. The first is to use a leader in the four to six foot range in a slightly lighter test than your main line from the rod. Attach the leader with a size seven black barrel swivel, include a size three bead above the barrel swivel. It is above this bead that your experimentation with weight begins. I use two types of weights, bass fisherman worm weights shaped like a bullet and regular drift fishing hollow core lead. These two types of weight allow line to pass through without damaging the line. The amount of weight to use is determined by the type of water you fish. Faster water requires more weight. The second method is to use a sliding jet diver above the plug, the leader length should be at least four to six feet to obtain necessary plug action. It is important to use the jet diver with a sliding technique rather than having the plug attached straight to the jet diver. The slider will allow for greater plug action.

Additional methods to keep plugs down and working are to add lead tape to various spots on the plug or lead wire to the shank of the front hook if you fish the plug with the front hook on. Rubber core or twist on sinkers along with split shot placed four to five feet above the plug are also recommended methods. Removal of the pivoting eye attachment ring, bending and backing out of the screw eye itself is also something to experiment with. Manufacturers of these plugs are experimenting with screw eye positioning and hook set ups to improve the diving ability of their plugs. Repositioning the screw eyes at a steeper angle by the manufacturers will eliminate previously mentioned methods for keeping these plugs down and working. Locating plugs with the repositioned eye screw in your local sporting goods store is difficult. When manufacturers have depleted their current stocks you will find more of these plugs with repositioned eye screws.

The additional requirements needed to get these plugs to run consistently are time consuming but once these plugs are properly tuned you have a great fish catcher.

I have found Wiggle Wart plugs to have considerably more tuning problems. I suspect this is because its lip and body design creates a greater horizontal motion in the current than its rival Hot Shot. Again, remember on Wiggle Wart plugs to use a Hot Shot snap. To correct poor-running Wiggle Warts and Tadpollys a different approach is needed. The Wiggle Wart and Tadpolly are manufactured without a solid line tie. When these plugs do not run correctly, it is usually due to a bent line-tie eyelet. If the line-tie eyelet is straight and the plug still runs off in one direction use the same process as for the Hot Shot and bend the line-tie eyelet a little in the opposite direction that the plug is running. Be careful not to damage the line-tie eyelet, it is not heavy enough to withstand a lot of applied pressure. Too much adjusting and bending will weaken the eyelet and you may lose a fish some time down the road. Do not fish any plug if the line-tie eyelet is loose, retire it to your plug hall of fame.

Constant checking of the attachment eyelet on the Wiggle Wart and Tadpolly and the screw eye on the Hot Shot, Flat Fish and Kwikfish for any movement or relocation is necessary, especially after a fish has been caught on the plug. In the process of fighting a steelhead the eye takes a lot of abuse. It is also necessary to check the hook screws and split rings for proper placement and condition not only after fighting a fish but periodically just for maintenance. This may sound like a time consuming routine but it's easy to pass up in the heat of battle when you're in a hurry to get the plug back out after having caught a fish.

A story that brings plug maintenance to mind happened a few years ago while I was fishing on the Siletz River on the central Oregon coast. This particular day I had the opportunity to fish with Dave Schamp who is recognized in the Northwest for his past involvement in the *Association of Northwest Steelheaders*. This recognition extends from his devotion to the preservation of salmon and steelhead along with his being a teacher of angling etiquette as well. On a personal basis I consider him to be a true professional in fishing plugs for steelhead. On this day of fishing the Siletz we discovered that we were fishing a plug without any hooks! We had failed to give attention to the plug's condition after Dave hooked and lost a fish. Dave is a true professional in the art of plug fishing for steelhead but even he cannot catch them without a hook! I am an avid supporter of catch and release but I like to play the fish for a period of time also. I had found, from fishing the Siletz for many years, an inconspicuous spot where fish hold just above a riffle. The bummer was that it was just below a popular boat ramp and I did not want to show all my coastal pals where it was. It always seemed to have a fish for me first thing in the morning. To avoid identifying the spot I would put the boat in before daylight, get on the spot and fish at first light. As others were just putting in we could barely see our plug rods working when Dave's rod went off and our first fish was on at an early point in the day. We proceeded to lose the fish at the net and being in a hurry simply threw the plug back out to try and hook another fish. After calling it quits some 20 minutes later we discovered Dave was fishing without any hooks on his plug. Luckily, we had no other strikes which would have resulted in non-hooked fish. The steelhead that Dave had hooked had somehow worked the hook and split ring off the plug. This unfortunate problem cannot be anticipated but can be somewhat controlled by making sure the screw eyes are turned tight into the plug and that all split rings are free of any gaps to eliminate the possibility of the ring catching on the hook eye or the screw eye and working free on a twisting fish. Obviously, if any hooks are bent they need to be replaced or straightened out depending on the severity of the bend. On fish catching plugs always replace hooks with the identical size and color.

Using substitutes has been known to eliminate the plug's fish catching ability and to keep the plug from obtaining hall of fame status.

Plug manufacturers believe that their plugs come properly tuned and if they do not that a little work will get the plug to produce the desired action. I have found some plugs never tune no matter what you try. These unfortunate few are reserved for another purpose in Chapter 7–Designing Your Own Colors and Patterns. Luhr–Jensen and Storm Lures will replace any plug that is defective due to water leakage inside the plug caused by the manufacturer. If this happens, put the plug in your freezer for 24 hours then place it in hot water upon which time air bubbles should be present. When purchasing plugs it is important to make a visual check before you leave the store. Make sure the plug's shape is contoured and smooth with no indications of poor gluing. Areas that have not been sanded smooth, especially on the lip of the plug's bill, will have an effect on the plug's performance.

6
Hook Set Ups

Nothing is more disappointing than missing the only strike of the day because of improperly prepared hooks. Remember to keep hooks razor sharp.

Plugs fished straight from the package catch fish but it is the goal of most steelhead fishermen to land every fish that is hooked. This is what I strive for even though I know it is not possible. For this reason I have found it necessary to change a few things. The point is not to take every fish home but there is that feeling of enjoyment in seeing face-to-face the fish which you have tried so hard and spent so much time in catching. My fondest memories of steelhead fishing are when I land these big and beautiful fish and then have the opportunity to slide it, with my own hands, back into the water, allowing it to return on its journey.

It is getting tougher every year to catch our friend the steelhead. Fishery management problems, coupled with the fact that my fishing days seem to get fewer and fewer each year are the reasons. My two main fishing companions, Dave and Dan, (no, not the decathletes) have a belief that good fishermen do not get skunked, they just run out of daylight and time. Let's face it, there are very few of us who get to fish as much as we would like. Those of us who are not fishing guides or who don't have an occupation that allows us to fish every time the river is in optimum shape, must take full advantage of every day and hour we are on the river. This means doing what is necessary to improve the odds of hooking and landing more fish. To catch fish you need hooks, the correct hooks, and on plugs the correct hook set up which will allow you to catch fish that strike your plug. To increase fish strikes to solid fish hookups I find it necessary to change not only the type of hook on various plugs but also to adjust the distance of the hook from the plug. These adjustments in type of hook and hook set up have produced better ratios between steelhead strikes and hookups. There is nothing more frustrating to a steelhead fisherman than to have a violent fish strike, or what I call a take down, on a plug and have the fish not be there when you come back on the rod. Doing everything correct–from being on the right river at the right time, fishing the correct spot, using the right plug with the correct presentation–only to see the rod go down for the first time in a long hard fished day and then pull back to have nothing, is enough to drive a plug fisherman off the deep end. How a steelhead can get its mouth on a plug without a hook sticking I do not know but it does happen. This brings me to the methods I have incorporated to remedy this problem.

The information I present on hooks and hook set ups has not been scientifically proven to improve your strike to hookup ratio, I present them only as ideas that have worked for me and others with whom I fish. The following plugs are the only ones in which adjustments are necessary to obtain better fish hookups.

The size 30 Hot Shot needs work, it does not have enough distance from the hook attachment screw in the belly to the hook itself. One can determine if a hook set up on a plug with a belly hook provides enough length by the following: Push the hook set up to the belly of the plug and measure the distance from the end of the plug to the tip of the upper hook on the treble hook. The distance between the hook tip and the end of the plug should be at least 1/2 an inch and not more than 3/4 of an inch from the back of the plug.

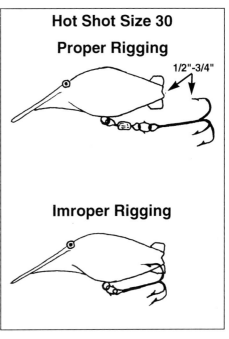

Even though the hook system hangs out away from the plug as it dives in the current, anything less than 1/2 an inch does not give a striking fish enough room to get a hook in the mouth. The fish is confronted with too much plastic. If a fish happens to strike when the current is not causing the bill of the plug to dig into the water at a severe angle the treble hook will ride against the bottom of the plug. As a result one of the three hooks is usually pushed against the plug in any type of fish strike. This gives the fish only two hooks, instead of three, with very little room to get the two hooks that are exposed.

Luhr-Jensen manufactures the size 30 plug with their special 9270 oval split ring, which gives some added distance but not enough. The plug comes equipped with a 2X strong treble hook which is a good quality hook that I have had no problems with. The VMC 9649 is the treble to use. I have found two successful methods to improve upon the hook system of the size 30 Hot Shot. The method I choose to run on the plug is determined by what type of hook I want to fish, treble or siwash. Since most rivers in Oregon are now under barbless hook regulations for the preservation of our wild fish I have been using mostly siwash hooks on the size 30 Hot Shot. The results have been great in getting solid hooks into fish that strike the plug. Most fish hooked with the siwash have been hooked in the nose or top of the mouth, this is because the hook rides in the water with the hook tip pointing up at the tail of the plug.

To change the size 30 Hot Shot for fishing with a lengthened treble hook system a little work is needed. First, remove the oval split ring and the treble hook from the belly screw eye with some split ring pliers. Then, remove the belly screw eye from the Hot Shot with a pair of needle nose pliers. Place the screw eye on a flat surface, preferably not your wife's kitchen table, open the eye of the screw enough to slip a size 7 barrel swivel inside the eye. Choose a barrel swivel color that best matches the plug, these swivels can be found in the three colors, brass/copper, chrome and black. I have found the easiest method to open the eye of the screw is with a small screw driver with a tip that will fit into the gap remaining in the eye. Filing down the tip on an old screw driver works well for this purpose.

Lay the screw eye down flat on a piece of wood and place the screw driver in the gap of the eye, apply pressure on the screw driver until the eye opens to the amount needed. By flipping the screw eye over once a small gap is created, applying pressure again from the opposite side seems to make the going a little easier. Once you have the desired gap size, place the barrel swivel in the eye and reclose the gap with needle nose pliers. Place the screw

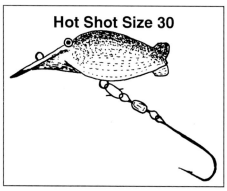

Hot Shot Size 30

back into the belly of the plug until the screw eye is tight against the plug with the gap facing the front lip of the plug. This will prevent the swivel from riding in the gap of the screw eye.

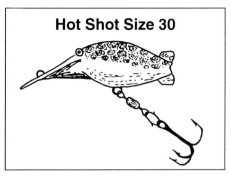

Hot Shot Size 30

Next, place the oval split ring onto the barrel swivel and attach your treble hook. This system really helps when a fish has been hooked and is fighting with a constant rotating, twisting motion. The barrel swivel lets the hook turn with the fish rather than twisting in the fishes mouth to eventually pull out. I have experienced this unfortunate hook release when trying to use two or three oval split rings in attempt to add length, instead of using a barrel swivel.

To fish the size 30 Hot Shot with a siwash system you need to remove the treble hook from the oval split ring on the belly and add a size seven barrel swivel to the oval split ring. The next step is to attach your brand choice of size 1 siwash hook to the barrel swivel. I recommend the VMC 9171. This hook provides plenty of strength needed for a siwash hook. The largest hook I recommend running on the size 30 is a 1/0. A larger siwash puts the hook at too great a distance behind the plug, reducing its effectiveness and action.

If you decide to run the size 30 Hot Shot with a size 1/0 hook, again a different type of hook system is recommended. A hook system like the one explained for the lengthened treble hook should be used. The only adjustment is to not include an oval split ring on the open end of the barrel swivel, which is attached to the belly screw eye. Instead, attach your choice for a size 1/0 siwash. Again, I recommend the VMC 9171. It is my opinion that whenever

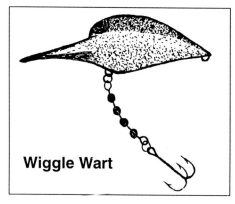

Wiggle Wart

you run a plug with a siwash hook the siwash should be attached to a barrel swivel. This allows the siwash to run behind the plug with the hook point facing up and not out to one side or another causing the plugs action to be affected. Like mentioned previously this also produces more hookups in the nose and upper mouth were the hook is less capable of working loose.

The other Hot Shot that I modify is the size 40. With this plug, I change the size three split ring that comes on the plug with a 9270 oval split ring. The 9270 is the same size oval split ring that comes on the size 30. This change is solely for the purpose of adding a little length to the hook system.

On the Wiggle Wart series each size needs a change in the hook system and on some plugs the hook itself. With Wiggle Wart plugs I run a hook system from the belly hook attachment eyelet. The first order of duty no matter what size of Wiggle Wart you're using is to remove the hooks from the belly and the tail of the plug, leaving the split ring on the belly eyelet only.

The Pee Wee Wart, the smallest in the series, comes with hooks too small for our friend the steelhead so discard both the tail and belly hooks. Leave the split ring on the belly eyelet but remove the split ring from the from the tail eyelet. On the remaining split ring attach a size seven barrel swivel. Attach the split ring you removed from the tail eyelet to the bottom eye of the barrel swivel and then attach a size 4 treble hook. I recommend the VMC 9648 which is manufactured barbless.

The system I recommend for the Wee Wart and Wiggle Wart (it also works well on the 1/2 ounce SE Hot Shots) are the same, with the exception of hook size. To change the hook system on these two plugs first remove the hook from the belly eyelet leaving the split ring, then remove the split ring and hook from the tail eyelet. On the remaining belly split ring attach a size 4 beaded chain swivel. These swivels are rated for 75 pounds and are 1 1/4 inches in length. On the end of the beaded chain swivel attach the split ring you removed from the tail eyelet. On the split ring attach a size 4 treble to the Wee Wart and a size 3 treble to the Wiggle Wart. To fish the Wee Wart and Wiggle Wart with a siwash hook disregard the bottom split ring from the beaded swivel and attach a size 1 siwash to the Wee Wart and a size 1/0 to the Wiggle Wart.

The change I recommend for the smaller sized Flat Fish and Kwikfish is to remove the belly hook completely. Specifically, those sizes below K12 and U20 for which I have found the belly hook to be a nuisance. With both hooks on the plug they have a tendency to hook together. The K12 and U20 hooks will not hook together if the split ring from the belly hook is removed and the hook reattached to the screw eye. The removal of the belly hook does not seem to reduce fish hookups on the smaller sizes.

Make sure that no matter what hook set up you choose your hook or hooks are razor sharp. Hooks should be sticky to the touch. Do not hesitate to replace hooks that have lost their point. Again, replace them with the identical size and color.

7
Designing Your Own Colors and Patterns

Customizing plugs with an airbrush can be a fun and rewarding hobby. The author shows off what this sport is all about.

I have found success over the years fishing plugs where I created the color or color pattern.

This idea is not one I can take total credit for. A few years back, during the development of a fishing friendship, I noticed my new fishing friend had some very unique colors and color patterns on a few of his plugs. I knew these plugs were not available from any manufacturer. Upon questioning, he admitted that he experimented with a few and found that they did work. This idea sparked my interest because I enjoy working and experimenting with my plugs in some fashion or another.

I compare the process of designing your own plug

colors to that of designing spinners for steelhead and salmon. There is great enjoyment in designing a plug you think might catch fish and after a try on the river learn your fishing instincts were correct. I have always had success with white clown corkies with red dots on one of my favorite coast rivers. Finding these desired colors and patterns only in trout size plugs, I created my own version on a size 30 Hot Shot. This plug joyously produced fish like I thought it might.

The process of painting your own plugs is easy and relatively inexpensive. Purchase a cheap air brush to make your designs look professional. An air brush that uses a replaceable air canister is a good choice and is less expensive because it doesn't require a compressor. These air brushes spray almost any kind of paint you can buy. Some however require a little added thinner. A can of spray paint also works for this purpose but seems to make a bigger mess. A tool to hold plugs while painting and drying is necessary. Find a holding tool from the jewelry or fly tying world with alligator clips and a heavy base.

When you start on the painting process make sure to use common sense regarding ventilation and safety. Once plugs have been painted with your desired colors they can be dried quickly with a hair dryer. Again, use care around flammables! Another item one can use when designing plugs is the Sharpie pen. These pens come in a variety of colors and are permanent once dry. I have also found Fishermun's Lure-Coat to be handy. Dipping the plug into this product has produced some great variations in plated/metallic-colored plugs that you may want. If you choose to dip plugs it is a good idea to remove all screw eyes to prevent them from becoming clogged, especially plugs that have a tuning screw eye.

As you can imagine designing your own plugs can

be an endless process, do not go crazy at first. Design a few and give them a chance to be fish catchers. Use those plugs that you couldn't tune for practice in the painting process before purchasing plugs strictly for designing.

Even if you choose not to get into designing your own colors and patterns on plugs, I recommend doing some work on the eyes of plugs, particularly Hot Shots. Wiggle Warts come with very pronounced eyes and needs no improvement. I believe this adds to a more realistic looking plug that will cause more fish to strike. I usually add some white Lure-Coat with a tooth pick to the eye. This not only makes the eye stand out in color but also in size. Once dry, color the pupil in your choice of Sharpie pen.

Proper storage of plugs is often overlooked. To preserve the finish on your plug collection line the storage trays of your plug box with some type of soft carpet material. This will cushion the plugs while riding in the boat or truck and prevent them from rubbing against a hard surface, scratching and dulling your collection. The Plano 757 or 787 are good sized tackle boxes and each hold over 100 plugs in an organized fashion. Plug organization is key when your collection is in the hundreds. Sort drawers by size and trays by color patterns to allow for quick retrieval.

⑧
Choosing the Right Plug

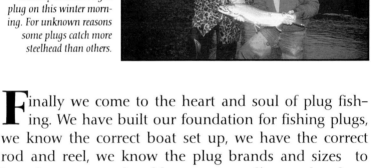

The author (left) and noted steelhead angler Buzz Ramsey chose the right plug on this winter morning. For unknown reasons some plugs catch more steelhead than others.

Finally we come to the heart and soul of plug fishing. We have built our foundation for fishing plugs, we know the correct boat set up, we have the correct rod and reel, we know the plug brands and sizes to keep in our arsenal and how to properly tune the plugs. We must now learn which plug to choose and how to fish it correctly, this is the hard part!

There are a few plug fishermen who do not believe there is such a thing as choosing the correct plug, they feel there is only one plug. The fishermen who subscribe to this notion fish day after day with the same old plug, knowing that the plug they are fishing is a fish catcher. I have heard rumors of a few plug fishermen who have a single plug in their arsenal which has caught over 200 steelhead. The only way a plug is going to catch 200 fish is for that plug to be fished, fished and always fished regardless of water conditions. I am not saying this is incorrect, I believe there are some plugs that catch fish and others that will not, regardless of the size, brand and color. As much as I would like to follow this approach, I cannot bring myself to fish only one plug, even if the plug has a great fish catching record. When a plug gets to the point where it has caught five or six fish I begin to classify it as a "Hall of Famer." Once I have a plug in this category I fish another that is exactly like it, for two purposes. The first reason is that I get nervous about losing a fish catching plug, nothing tears me up more than losing a fish catching plug in a root left over from a recent high water. Plugging uncharted river sections or new rivers is also a great opportunity to say good bye to your winner. When fishing new sections of water or new rivers fish a plug you don't mind losing or as my fishing buddies say a plug your not "married to."

Second, I like to find out if it is the color or just the uniqueness of that individual plug that makes it a fish catcher. If you happen to catch fish on the plug's twin the question is still there but you have gained another fish catching plug. Losing a plug that has caught only one or two fish will not sting near as much as losing a plug which has caught 200 fish! You could say I am a pessimist, or you may think I have two left arms on the oars, but this is not the case. I enjoy developing a collection of fish catching plugs and believe it is a better option than the one plug society. If a plug fisherman fishes only one plug he will always wonder if he could have caught fish if he had used a different plug that better matched the water conditions or had been a better match for a particular piece of water. A plug fisherman that has developed, over time, an arsenal of plugs that catch fish will be able to match the water conditions or the uniqueness of a particular piece of water with a plug that he knows catches fish.

If you are a member of the "one plug society" you can skip ahead to the proper rigging of plugs. For those who feel the "variety society" is for you, continue. There are many factors that need to be considered when choosing the correct plug. We begin with the condition of the water you are fishing. The fish's ability to see your plug is related to water clarity. If fish cannot see your plug it is not the ideal situation. The plug's vibration (even without a rattle) will move a fish towards your plug and possibly even tempt a steelhead to strike but not as often, nor as aggressively, as if the fish could see your plug in combination with feeling the vibration or that sweet tuned song.

When water clarity is poor, visibility of under four feet, using a larger sized plug with a rattle is vital. The added noise and vibration of the plug with a rattle will attract more fish to your plug. When the water has a visibility of over four feet, but is not clear enough to see the bottom, a rattle is a matter of personal choice. Although I believe the rattle is an advantage because fish are not easily spooked in this type of water. The addition of a rattle in these water conditions can be a critical factor in steelhead treating plugs as invaders of their territory. The rattle steps up the annoying factor in my opinion.

Even though steelhead can find their way to your plug in off color water by feeling the plug's vibration, it is essential that steelhead can locate the plug by sight. The fluorescent glow colors with metallic blue and gold or these colors in combination with others colors, used on rattle models have been found to produce fish consistently in poor visibility conditions. Usually when water is at a higher level as a result of a recent freshet of rain, visibility is poor.

In high water and poor visibility conditions I recommend the Wiggle Wart and size 25 and 35 in the Hot Shot series. Because of the large size of the 25 Hot Shot ample current is needed because of the plug's buoyancy. For water conditions in the middle range of visibility and water level, or what I call optimum conditions, when the color is steelhead green, choosing a plug is more difficult. In optimum river conditions I have found Hot Shots in sizes 30 and 35 to be the best producers. The depth of water in the section of river you choose to fish may also determine your choice in size. The size 35 runs down to 18 feet and the size 30 down to 12 feet.

When the rivers are low and clear smaller plugs are the way to go. When the water has enough clarity to see the bottom from any depth, small is the rule. A smaller plug will not spook fish and still entices a vicious strike. Hot Shot's in size 40 without a rattle are an excellent choice and so is the Pee Wee Wart. Luhr–Jensen has publicized the crawfish color pattern as a good low water color in the size 40 and they are right, it is a definite plug to have, especially if you find one with a darker paint job. To find a darker outcast, compare the plug to its brothers of the same pattern. You will notice slight variations in color among the family of plugs. The shrimp and rainbow trout patterns are also a good choice for low, clear water. In the Pee Wee Wart the blue scale/red lip has a good reputation.

Here are other fish catchers that worked over the last few steelhead seasons. Early in the year the cop car (black and white) and mother of pearl color patterns are good. The gold with fire top has been an excellent plug for the last few years, along with the metallic pink used during the peak season. The blue pirate is a proven fish catching color pattern with many of my plug fishing friends. Towards the spring of the season the white with red head Hot Shot is interesting to big native fish upon their arrival.

Size 40 Hot Shot and Pee Wee Wart plugs are again an excellent choice for plugging the smaller streams like those found on our Pacific coast. By small I mean those streams that are barely navigable by drift boat even after rain. Both plugs are 1/5 ounce and are ideal for the smaller, generally shallower streams. Colors that are good producers in the smaller streams are crawfish, metallic green, metallic gold, copper clad and white/black cop car in the Hot Shot line, with the metallic blue scale/red lip in the Pee Wee Wart also being a good producer. When these smaller streams are running a bit off color using a rattle in these small plugs is not out of the question. Generally, in these smaller streams using a rattle can be overkill because your plugs will likely be in the path of a fish. There is not much room for fish to hide from plugs in these small streams.

In stretches of river that are slow, the Flat Fish and Kwikfish have proven to be effective fish catchers. Again, the plug size best for back trolling for steelhead are in the 2 1/2 to 3 1/4 inch range in length and 5.5 grams to 8.5 grams in weight. Luhr-Jensen targets the K10 and K12 primarily for steelhead. The K12 will dive much deeper than the K10. These plugs need to be fished in slower and/or slow, deep water. Believe it or not, fluorescent red has been a top producing plug in low, clear water for some reason. Theory has it that it should spook fish but it does not. This may be due to the unique action of these plugs. In other types of water, gold has been a reliable producer.

It is important to remember that not all plugs are fish catchers so if you have plugs in these colors and patterns and have not been successful it may be that you need to try another. It is a good idea to have a few extras in proven colors and sizes in case of an unforeseen accident where a plug is lost either in a fish, or worse, our friend the root wad. I am not recommending that you have two of every plug, just those you have caught a good number of fish on. Like I mentioned previously, by adding proven plugs you develop a line of fish catchers which allows you to fish two or three proven plugs of the same model and color if you so choose. Nobody likes to fork out money for more plugs of the same color and size but pick up a few when they are on sale and you will not regret it. It just might be the one to catch fish for you down the road.

The use of scent on plugs for the purpose of masking human odor is optional. There are many scents on the market to choose from, do not use an expensive brand as it is not necessary. Shrimp scent has been effective, regardless of the plug or river being fished.

Marking plugs that catch fish is a practice I have found useful. Plugs that are fish catchers can be marked with a fish file on the back tail section or on the sides, either on the top or bottom. Each time the plug catches a fish, file another notch. Care should be taken not to file too deep into the plug, filing through the plug's shell will produce a leaker and possibly affect its fish catching characteristics. Otherwise notches do not interfere with the performance of the plug in any way. Notching in this manner makes the fish catchers easier to identify in comparison to the plug's brothers and sisters who look alike in your box. The statistics of the plug will be obvious and may influence the plug you choose to fish or its time of retirement.

I have provided you with some examples of plugs that work in various water conditions but you still need to experiment and develop your own line of fish producers. There is no guarantee that any specific plug will catch fish for everyone, plugs need to be tested and proved, sizes and colors can be suggested but the rest is up to you.

On the following pages I have provided a chart that will help in matching plugs to water conditions, along with the type of day (sunny or cloudy), to guide your decision making. This chart does not take into account the uniqueness of the section of river you are fishing which may also influence your choice.

Plug Selection Guide		
Water Conditions	**Plug**	**Color**
High, poor visibility, Brown/Green color	Hot Shot sizes 25, 35 with rattle	Glows/Fluorescents Chartreuses/Fires Coppers/Blues
	Wiggle Wart	Met. Blue/Red Specks Met. Hot Green Specks Met. Copper Copper Clad Gold/Fluor. Red Stripe
Optimum, fair visibility, Emerald/Steelhead Green	Hot Shot sizes 35, 30 Rattle Optional	Cop Car Mother of Prl Blk Head Met. Pink Green Double Eagle Gold Fire Top Silver/Blue Top Pirate Silver/Blue Bk Copper Plate
	Kwikfish/Flatfish Sizes K10, K12, U20	Fluorescent Red Fire Flame Red Gold/Copper Hot Head Slv/Grn/Chrt Met. Pink
	Wee Wiggle Wart	Met Cop/Grn Scale/Red Lip Met Blue Scale/Red Lip
	Tadpolly Size X9000	Gold Red Head Copper Red Head Met. Red
Low, clear water	Hot Shot Size 40, rattle in cold water	Crawfish Cop Car Shrimp Copper Met. Dark Green Gold/Green Pirate Rainbow Trout
	Pee Wee Wart	Blue Scale/Red Lip

Sky	Water Conditions	Plug	Color
Cloudy	Medium to low with fair visibility	Hot Shot 35, 30, 40	Painted
		Kwikfish/Flatfish K10, K12, U20	Painted
Prt Cld/Sunny		Hot Shot 35, 30, 40	Paint/Met. Combo
		Flatfish/Kwikfish	Paint/Met. Combo
Sunny		Hot Shot 35, 30, 40	Metallic
		Flatfish/Kwikfish	Metallic
		Tadpolly	Metallic

9
Proper Rigging

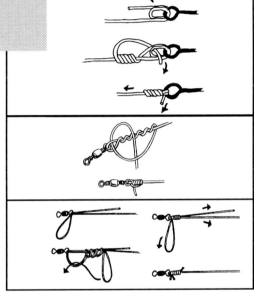

Knots essential to plug fishing are from top: trilene knot, improved clinch knot and double improved clinch knot.

To consistently hook fish by back trolling plugs from a drift boat, proper rigging is important. The first essential item is a size seven black barrel swivel. Attach the swivel to the end of your main line. Then add your choice of leader, in the five to seven foot range, to your Hot Shot round eye snap. There are several important reasons for the barrel swivel's use. First, the barrel swivel allows a hooked fish to spin or rotate freely eliminating any added tension to the plug's hooks and preventing line twist. Second, the length of leader between the barrel swivel and the plug prevents inexperienced fish fighters from reeling the plug to near the tip of the rod. This will result in a lost fish because too little line between the rod tip and the fish dramatically reduces the rod's ability to abate the fish's struggle for freedom. The size seven barrel swivel will stop at most rod tips and give the amount of room needed to glide a fish into the net, or give some extra coaching to your fishing companion. A note of caution here, too long a leader will increase the difficulty in bringing the fish to the net. My belief is, you're better off having trouble getting it to the net due to extra leader than having the fish break off while struggling because of lack of leader. The third reason is that in dirty water conditions the barrel swivel can be placed a bit closer (four to five feet) and used to reduce garbage build up (leaves, trash, etc) on the plug with the addition of a thick rubber band tied through the upper loop of the swivel. A piece of the rubber band should stick out one to two inches from each side of the loop. The rubber band will not catch all the garbage but will lengthen the plug's running time before the action is effected. A barrel swivel also allows the use of a leader with a different pound test than the main line. This may be nec-

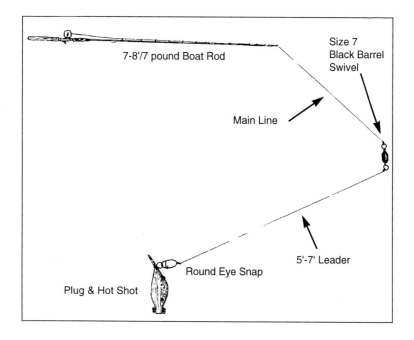

essary depending on water conditions. A beaded chain swivel also works in place of the barrel swivel when fishing large plugs but has the ability to be reeled in through the tip of the rod. If plugging with a rod that has a tip too large to stop a swivel it will be necessary to use a standard blood knot to attach the leader otherwise you are asking for problems. This is the case with Fenwick's LP 767C plug rods, they are manufactured with large rod tips. One can choose to replace the large tip with a smaller version or use a blood knot to attach the leader and lose the benefits a swivel provides.

Use of the Hot Shot round eye snap is critical, it should be attached to the leader by an improved clinch knot. Do not use an ordinary snap swivel to attach any plug. Its use will drastically reduce the intended fish catching action of the plug. Plugs which prohibit the use of a round eye snap (Pee Wee Wart and the Wee Wiggle Wart) should be attached to the leader line as suggested by the manufacturer. When attaching the round eye snap to the plug make sure the crossbar of the snap is facing up. If the snap is installed with the crossbar down it can catch on the plug's bill, effecting action and damaging the finish.

10
Fishing Your Plugs

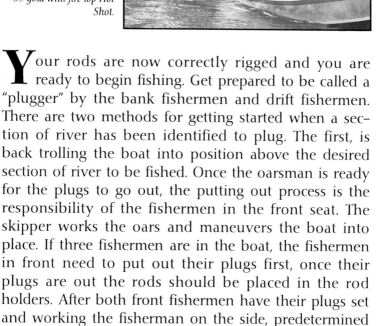

Dan Kern nets a Siletz River steelhead for the author. The fish hit the Siletz River special, a size 35 gold with fire top Hot Shot.

Your rods are now correctly rigged and you are ready to begin fishing. Get prepared to be called a "plugger" by the bank fishermen and drift fishermen. There are two methods for getting started when a section of river has been identified to plug. The first, is back trolling the boat into position above the desired section of river to be fished. Once the oarsman is ready for the plugs to go out, the putting out process is the responsibility of the fishermen in the front seat. The skipper works the oars and maneuvers the boat into place. If three fishermen are in the boat, the fishermen in front need to put out their plugs first, once their plugs are out the rods should be placed in the rod holders. After both front fishermen have their plugs set and working the fisherman on the side, predetermined by the oarsman, needs to put out the bonus rod for the skipper. When using this order tangles will be prevented. With the skipper and only one front seater the process is simplified because each rod has a side.

The second method of getting started is from an

anchored position. When using this method it is necessary to anchor far above the section of river that one desires to fish. Starting from the anchored position is, at times, not as easy as one would think. This method of starting gets complicated when the oarsman begins to pull the anchor up. At this point the current will begin turning the boat in one direction or another. This turning action can cause the plugs below the boat to cross one another and tangle. I have witnessed many plug fishermen not experienced in this starting process demonstrate this problem, especially where there is a fair amount of current. One should never anchor in deep, fast or boily water for safety reasons.

There are some ways to prevent the turning of the boat during the anchor raising process. One is to make sure the drift boat is in the middle of any horizontal swing in the current. Second, when the boat begins to turn, dig the corresponding oar in the water to correct the swing. Keep in mind that the boat will swing when starting from an anchored position. After experiencing a three plug tangled up a few times you remember the drift boat turns in the process of raising the anchor and you become skilled in taking the required corrective actions. When starting from an anchored position each fisherman can be responsible for putting out their own rod, including the oarsman.

It is of paramount importance to run plugs below the boat at the same distance, this is especially true when only two plugs are being fished. Plugs vibrating and creating the tuned song while abreast are more likely to irritate a fish and cause it to strike one of the plugs. If fishing three plugs, the third plug is typically the oarsman's rod set behind the front seat, it is necessary to run that plug a bit shorter than the two front plugs. Shortening the back plug will help prevent tangles when maneuvering the drift boat. If three plugs are being run from rods located in the front of the boat, the middle plug should be lengthened slightly (1' to 2') in front of the other two. Do not play the game that the farthest plug out gets the fish, this selfish ploy reduces the fish striking irritation that a gang of plugs produces.

The distance the plugs should be run below the boat is dependent upon water clarity and the oarsman's ability to maneuver. I recommend a maximum distance of 60 feet, no further. This provides adequate room from the boat and allows for good plug maneuverability. It is a common mistake to let out too much line. Plugs that are run too far from the boat are difficult to swing over desired fish holding spots. The ability to control the plug is reduced as distance from the boat is increased. It then takes more time to cover the intended section because the plug's reaction to the boat is delayed due to line length.

There are many methods of identifying the proper distance of the plug from the boat. The most popular is to count the number of times the line guide crosses the spool of the reel (bait casting). Another common method is to add a bobber stopper knot made from red thread at the desired distance point. When the red knot comes through the tip of the rod the plug is out the correct distance. The last method is to use Dacron line on the reel spool and attach the correct length of monofilament. The plug is let out to the Dacron monofilament splice.

Once the plugs are out and working and the oarsman has the boat maneuvering into position the front seat fisherman can relax and enjoy some coffee. The oarsman or skipper now has to do all the work. The drift boat needs to be held back (back trolled) in the current at a pace that causes the plugs to dig down against the current and run with the intended tuned action. The proper pace downriver can be determined

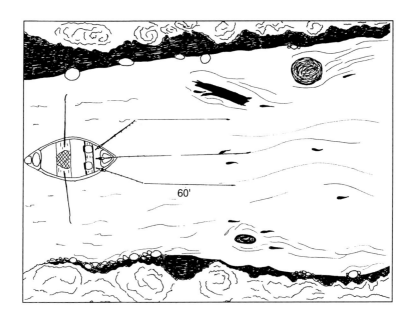

by the action of the rod tip. As a plug dives and wiggles the rod tip will vibrate, emulating the plug's action beneath the water's surface. If the rod tip does not move the boat's pace is too fast downstream. In this case the oarsman needs to increase his effort on the oars or take bigger bites into the water to slow the drift boat's pace until the rod tips begin to vibrate. The pace the plugs are worked downstream is also very important in generating strikes from fish. The slower the pace, the more thoroughly one can cover a section of river. A slower paced plug will produce more strikes than a plug that comes zipping past a fish. A plug moving too fast does not represent the same threat a slow paced plug will. The oarsman should maneuver the drift boat left and right in a lateral fashion as the boat is worked downstream. This lateral maneuvering will cover more area and produce more fish.

The failure of the rod tip to vibrate may also be the cause of a "weed up". An accumulation of garbage (grass and leaves) has either stuck onto the bill of the plug or gathered on the hooks. The added garbage causes the plug's action to be lethargic or will cause the plug to roll to the water's surface. The weeded-up plug can be identified by the dead (nonvibrating) rod tip. A fish will not strike a plug that is weeded-up so it is necessary to identify and remedy the problem. A proven technique to remove grass from the plug, without reeling it up to the boat, is to give the plug an aggressive jerk. Remove the rod from the rod holder and point the rod tip straight at the plug below the boat in a position parallel to the water's surface. When the line is tight, use a quick jerk and force the rod tip back to a twelve o'clock position. Keep the butt of the rod in the same place throughout this process to provide a quick, sharp jerk from the tip. This aggressive jerk will generally remove all grass. This allows the grass to be removed without having to bring the plug to the boat, increasing your fishing time. Garbage removal will be indicated by the return of the desired rod tip action. When fishing with people new to plugging, it is a good idea to show them this technique at the start of the day and let them practice a few times. It also allows them to practice removing the rod from the holder and setting the hook. Often new plug fishermen tend to not pull the rod tip back with enough authority and speed needed to remove the grass.

When a fish has been hooked the oarsman should continue to row the drift boat until an adequate place can be found to anchor and fight the fish. Do not worry about other plugs remaining out below the boat until anchored, the hooked fish seldom gets tangled with these plugs. If three fishermen are in the boat, the free fishermen can reel in the plugs and allow the fisherman to enjoy the fight. When the oarsman is the sole fisherman in the boat and a fish strikes his plug there may become potential for an accident if not handled correct-ly. When fishing solo leave the plug rod in the holder until a suitable anchoring spot is located. The common mistake is to let the anchor fly when the fish strikes. Depending on the current this may be OK but often the current is strong enough to make fighting the fish back to the boat, along with the netting process, impossible for one person. The sole fisherman is better off giving the fish a quick hook set. This should be done by grab-bing the rod below the first eye and pulling back on the rod while the rod is still in the holder. Once the hook set is complete, row for the nearest site of relief to anchor and fight the fish. I have lost more fish by trying to anchor and set the hook at the same time then I have by leaving the rod in the holder until an adequate anchoring spot is found. When anchoring in faster water many fish are lost by working the fish back to the boat. This is impossible at times, especially with a large fish. The other potential for loss is trying to net the steelhead by yourself in fast current.

It is important to identify the origin of the fish (hatchery or native) as the fish nears the boat. The iden-tification of clipped fins will determine if the fish should be netted or released in the water. Native fish should not be netted or brought into the boat to thrash around. If a photo is desired, get out of the boat and land the fish on the bank where it can be kept in the water to avoid added stress.

The last point I would like to make in this chapter is in regard to plug fishing etiquette. When in the process of fishing plugs you happen to come upon bank fishermen or anchored drift fishermen make sure and pull your plugs in plenty short of their fishing envelope. Allowing the plugs to be back trolled near others who have established their territory can cause panic and hostility. Always go around on the bank side of any anchored drift boat and as close to the bank as possible when passing a bank fisherman. This will keep you out of their holding water and make life much easier for all who are on the river. Many fishermen with drift boats unfortunately do not follow this rule and give other boaters a bad reputation. I admit some people are never happy, no matter how you try to pass them. In this circumstance it is helpful to have a fishing friend in the front seat who is large in stature with a mean, angry look on his face. I am fortunate to often have a former Pac Eight defensive end in my front seat. Luckily, the only time he gets angry is when people make fun of our alma mater's win loss record.

11
Curtain of Death

A young John Turley shows off a Siletz steelhead taken from the water in the background. Teaching young people about steelhead fishing will help preserve the great fish for our future generations.

The curtain of death is an effective method of catching fish with the plugging technique. The curtain of death is simply that, a curtain of plugs going down the river irritating any fish it happens to run into. The curtain of death is a technique for two or more drift boats. Two drift boats back troll plugs abreast at a distance just far enough apart that their plugs will not tangle, slowly maneuvering downstream. This technique is great when fishing with friends but do not sneak in along another boat, they will probably not appreciate the invasion of their fishing space.

This technique was developed while fishing my boat with a fishing partner along with my friend Dave who would fish his boat with his partner. Often we would join up and talk about our day's success (or lack of). During these periods of conversation and lunch we would have our plugs abreast proceeding down the river. When running our plugs side by side in areas of rivers with ample room and desired current we always seemed to catch a fish. After some thought about our reason for success we incorporated the "curtain" technique in more sections of rivers with similar characteristics and found that it truly worked. It seems the fish get the Tillamook Bay craze where they see so many plugs coming at them no matter which way they turn so they strike in self defense! This is my theory as to why the guides catch so many Chinook in Tillamook Bay compared to most weekend anglers. The guides have so many spinners (4 to 6) in the water, compared to the common angler, the.r chances simply increase with numbers but there is the fish irritation or attraction that also increases with greater numbers. This factor is the key in my opinion.

The use of the curtain of death in the right section of river will allow fish that move laterally away from any plug to be confronted by or directed to another. The fish are backed downriver and at some point will decide to turn and go downstream or make an attempt to move up and around the irritation. Backing the fish down to a point above a rapid or riffle where they do not want to descend is ideal, the fish will often strike rather than descend the rapid.

The success of this technique has had a great effect on some of my fishing friends. They have witnessed this technique catch fish in the same location of the Siletz River on three consecutive trips. Sure, it could be the spot just holds fish but I have fished the same location enough to know the technique was a major factor in our success. The crazy thing is that each boat was aligned the same, the same plug was being fished and the same rod hooked the fish every time! Some may think this is a moving hog line in the making. I do not recommend using this technique all the way down the river but give it a try on sections where it permits. The curtain of death has been a certain producer for me.

12
Fish the Flats

Guide Clancy Holt helped clients hook this, and many other, steelhead while fishing the "flats" with a Hot Shot. When conditions are right plug fishing is more effective than any other method.

Identifying good plugging water is no different than locating prime drift fishing water. Plugs catch steelhead in almost any location of the river, it's just that there are sections of river that do not lend themselves to plugging. Some spots are either too deep or shallow, too slow or fast or too brushy. All of these factors have an effect on the oarsman's ability to pace the drift boat for proper plug action and presentation.

Sections of river that are ideal are those 3 to 14 feet in depth and with a current the speed of a brisk human walk or a little slower. The ordinary places that steelhead are often found are also a good choice. Riffle tailouts, parting lines and above the riffles are common places to find our friend the steelhead. Plugs take fish in these spots but I have found flats between riffles and rapids to be generally the most productive place to take fish. Flats which contain the correct depth and current allow for easy maneuvering of the drift boat for the oarsman and are often resting places for steelhead on their upstream journey. These flats can be worked thoroughly with plugs being presented at the slow desired pace. Upon hooking a fish in these flats, a calm eddy can usually be found and the problem of being taken downstream often avoided. The flats also let plug fishermen get two or three chances at more fish. Once a fish has been caught plugging a flat it is imperative that the flat be plugged again. The flat enables the oarsman to do this because generally on one side of the river or the other there is slower water that will allow the oarsman to row back upstream to repeat the process.

Once fish have been located in a flat put some time in and make several passes. It is not uncommon to catch another fish and sometimes more when additional passes are made. A general rule is that at least three passes should be made after a fish has been hooked. It is a common mistake not to do this. I have watched many pluggers hook a fish and just keep on going downriver with no pressure from other fishermen to go back. I have dropped in right behind them and slammed the fish they left behind. Thanks guys!

Rocks, pockets and cut banks are also good places to fish plugs, just remember what particular spot is coming up next and get everything ready to hit them. The best method in identifying these little one fish pockets is to observe the bottom of the river during low, clear water conditions and make note of spots you feel hold fish. Make a mental note or write them down. It is a good idea to mark a bank location by noting a tree or any other landmark that will survive a high water blow out. When the river is up with some color these spots are not as easy to identify and having something to remember them by will help. It is also important to remember where you saw other fishermen catch fish, plug fishermen or any other. Determine if the spot can be easily hit by a plug and fish it the next time down the river.

I like to share information on spots with my fishing friends, where fish have been caught or where I witnessed a fish caught. People who refuse to tell where they caught fish are greedy. They actually think that if you return to fish the spot they mentioned you might catch all the fish! Their common answer to the question "Where did you catch your fish?" is "In the water!" Sharing information on river locations that hold fish has provided me knowledge of many fish holding places I did not recognize or did not believe would hold fish. The reciprocated sharing of locations will help everyone catch more fish. I readily share information, especially with fishermen who catch and release.

High water conditions prohibit the plugging of normal spots. It is necessary to plug the current lines near the river's edge. Fish travel nearer the bank to stay out of the increased current and use the bank as a reference for navigation. Success will be found plugging these edges as the water begins to recede from higher levels rather than on the rising side. For some reason fish do not seem interested in a plug or much else in raising conditions. During low water levels the deeper side above riffles seem to attract steelhead. From this vantage point steelhead can view upcoming meals or threats and decide to retreat into the cover of the white broken surface water a few feet below.

13
Plugging Hazards

While keeping his ears warm the author attempts to net a fish solo. Fishing alone on occasion can be enjoyable.

Like any other type of steelhead fishing there are some hazards associated with the technique of plugging, especially if common sense is forgotten. Any time a fisherman is in a drift boat caution and safety is a must. Bill Luch's book, *Steelhead Drift Fishing,* has excellent information on drift boat safety and rapid navigation. It is a must for anyone who rows a drift boat. Plugging has some added factors in boating safety because the drift boat is generally always in motion, (unless the oarsman is taking a well needed break). Another factor is the plugs being run below the boat. It is important to keep in mind that a $5.00 plug is not worth losing human lives or a drift boat. If a problem situation should arise do not worry about saving the plugs, even if they are all fish catchers. Always correct the boat's situation first, then worry about the plugs!

There are common mistakes that seem to get plug fisherman in trouble. One is leaving rods in the holders when navigating rapids. The rods often have plugs incorrectly reeled to the tip. The rods can snag tree limbs as the current takes the drift boat down the deep side of a shallow rapid near the bank. Once the rod is snagged it will turn the drift boat in shallow water potentially causing a flip if the chine strikes the bottom or a rock. It is wise to place rods horizontally in the boat before running any riffle. Rod tips should be tucked inside the boat when maneuvering through any hazardous stretch of water. Low water escalates this problem as the condition eliminates the safe routes of passage through many rapids. This situation often brings the drift boat nearer the bank and overhanging trees. Another common mistake is trying to remove a snagged plug in a section of river that has a strong current. Fishermen leaning over the side of the drift boat swinging nets into the water to save their favorite plug is a common sight. Retrieving plugs in this type of water has the oarsman anchoring in a place he normally would not, often causing the anchor to be lost in the same mess that has snagged the plug. Plugging too far down into the top of a riffle from above can cause serious problems. The oarsman wants to plug right down to the top edge of the riffle just knowing a fish is ready to strike, having been pushed to the limit. Then, instead of hooking a fish a plug gets snagged in the fast water at the top of the riffle, making it difficult for the oarsman to position the drift boat in any safe manner to save the plug because the current is too strong. The drift boat enters the rapid or riffle in an undesirable position which could put all in danger.

Plugging by the oarsman without other fishermen in the boat can also be asking for trouble if caution is not used. When plugging alone in the drift boat select areas of the river which will not present problems when a fish is hooked. Choose river sections that provide an easy place to anchor and fight a fish without placing you in a dangerous situation. There are many other situations that can be dangerous but the use of common sense, along with not taking unnecessary chances and paying attention will eliminate most drift boat accidents.

14
Maneuvering with Ease

Remember in low, clear water conditions fish smaller plugs. This fish was taken in gin clear water with a size 40 Hot Shot.

As needed in the plugging process, the drift boat is always being rowed to create plug action. Many who begin to plug fail to realize the amount of rowing that takes place over a day of running plugs. When drift fishing, the drift boat is simply guided downstream to the next stop then anchored to fish the spot. The plug fisherman is constantly at the oars, no matter how easy the effort, it is constant.

The point of this chapter is to identify ways to minimize the effort of the oarsman regardless of how large the front seat fishermen are. Rowing a couple of large fishermen around all day can draw on your greatest strengths and nerves. Being an old tight end from the Pac Ten, I at one time felt I could row all day no matter who was in front. Times change and so has my stomach and I now find it not quite as easy as it used to be.

There are many things for the oarsman that can make the going difficult. The oarsman needs to coach the front seater, regardless of whether there is one or three, not to lean. Front seat fishermen leaning over the side to put out their plugs (or for any other reason) make it impossible for the drift boat to track and the oarsman to row in the desired direction with ease. It is of the greatest importance to keep the weight in the middle of the boat or what I refer to as "on the bubble". For those front seat fishermen who cannot figure this out place a bubble level between the knee braces on the fly deck. I have found a large RV level to be the best. Some people are visual learners! The bubble can be removed later without any damage to the boat's finish. The distribution of weight from front to back is also important in the drift boat's ability to track in the water. Too much forward weight creates an unnecessary plowing action as the oarsman back trolls. A heavy rear will cause the stern to dig into the water on the oarsman's stroke. Both improper weight distributions require unnecessary energy from the oarsman and are cause for early burnout.

15
Fish Others!

This trophy steelhead was taken from a section of deep, slow water with a gold K12 Kwikfish, water that other plugs were unable to fish effectively.

For all the enjoyment steelhead fishing has brought me over the years I feel a compelling need to help enhance the species. I want these fish to be around for my son. The best method to get people involved in the plight of the anadromous species is to take them fishing. No matter how young or old, once a person has caught a steelhead they want to repeat the opportunity. Taking people fishing and teaching them about steelhead, and fishing in general, will bring another soldier into the army for the preservation of the fish.

Being employed in the education profession I enjoy sharing steelhead fishing with young people. Teaching our youth fishing techniques and proper fishing etiquette is something all of us who fish must do. All steelhead fishermen cherish their time on the river and are somewhat selfish about it because we know the days are limited. I recommend sacrificing one Saturday out of the steelhead season to take a young person for a drift trip. Male or female they never will forget the day, regardless of whether fish are caught. You are provided with the opportunity to share stories and teach fishing etiquette, something there is never enough of. From that day forward a new fisherman will be hooked on the sport of steelhead fishing and you will have developed an eager fishing partner for those mornings when your regular front seater sleeps in and fails to rendezvous.

About the Author

Mike Laverty is a native Oregonian, born and raised in Newport, on the central Oregon coast. Mike grew up cutting cedar bolts, razor clam digging, hunting fowl, blacktail deer, Roosevelt elk and fishing. As a young boy his parents owned property along the Siletz River where he was introduced to summer and winter steelhead.

Continuing to fish throughout high school and his college football days at OSU, Mike would catch passes on Saturdays in Parker Stadium and salmon and steelhead Sundays on the Siletz. After college Mike entered the field of education, first as a teacher then as an administrator, where he takes every opportunity to share importance of the preservation of salmon, trout and steelhead.

Enjoying the opportunity to take his dad fishing, Mike started fishing plugs in an attempt to keep his father from becoming frustrated by the bird's nest blues. From years of fishing plugs as part of his steelheading arsenal, Mike began to identify techniques that consistently improved his plug fishing success.

When not in his drift boat or tinkering with his plugs, Mike enjoys cooking gourmet meals for his wife Heidi and telling his newborn son, Hayden, about the big fish that got away.